KOALA

Dylanna Press

Meet the Koala

Get ready to meet one of the coolest animals on Earth! Koalas are fuzzy, adorable mammals that hang out in the eucalyptus forests of eastern Australia. These unique creatures live only along the eastern and southern coasts of Australia—nowhere else on the planet! If you want to spot a wild koala, you'll have to travel to places like Queensland or South Australia.

Here's a surprise—koalas aren't bears at all! Even though people call them "koala bears," they're actually marsupials, just like kangaroos, wombats, and possums. Like their marsupial cousins, female koalas carry and nurse their babies in a pouch. Early European settlers thought they looked like bears, but they were totally wrong!

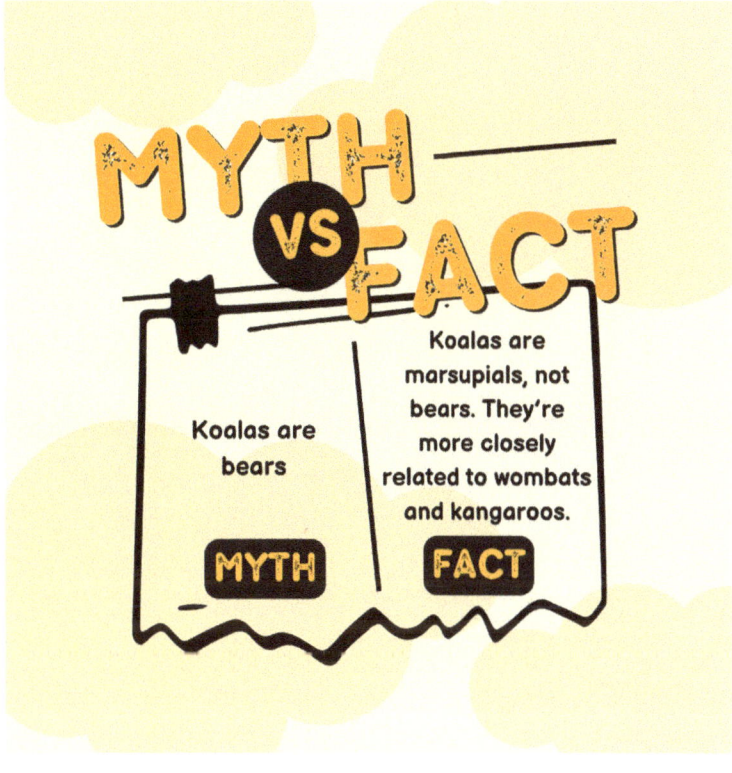

Their scientific name is *Phascolarctos cinereus*—try saying that three times fast! It comes from Greek words meaning "pouch bear" and Latin for "ash-colored" because of their gray fur.

Koalas are mega-famous worldwide and have become one of Australia's most recognized animal superstars! With their sleepy eyes and slow-moving ways, koalas might seem simple—but they're anything but. Get ready to find out more about these amazing animals.

_____
marsupials – mammals that carry their babies in a pouch

What Do Koalas Look Like?

Koalas look like living stuffed animals, with their round, fluffy ears, large black noses, and compact bodies covered in thick gray or brown fur. They're about the size of a small dog—measuring 24 to 33 inches (60 to 85 cm) tall and weighing between 9 and 33 pounds (4 to 15 kg). Males are usually larger than females and have a dark, shiny patch on their chest. This isn't just a marking—it's a scent gland used to mark trees and signal their presence to other koalas.

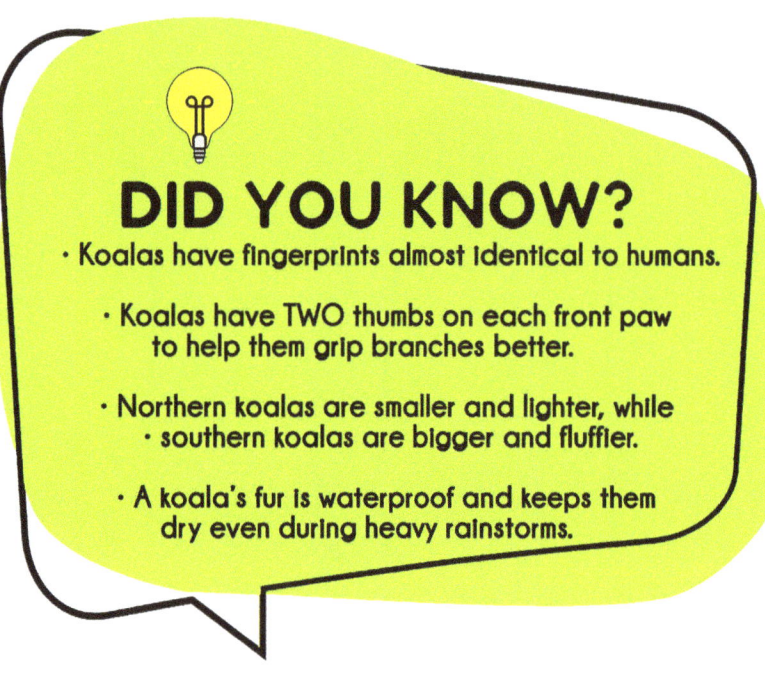

DID YOU KNOW?
- Koalas have fingerprints almost identical to humans.
- Koalas have TWO thumbs on each front paw to help them grip branches better.
- Northern koalas are smaller and lighter, while southern koalas are bigger and fluffier.
- A koala's fur is waterproof and keeps them dry even during heavy rainstorms.

Their sharp claws and strong limbs are perfect for life in the trees. Koalas have five digits on each front paw, and two of them act like thumbs, giving them extra grip for climbing and holding onto branches. On their back feet, they have a special grooming claw formed by two fused toes that helps them clean and maintain their thick fur.

Koalas' large, furry ears rotate to help detect sounds from different directions. Their eyes are small but spaced wide apart, giving them a broad field of vision to spot movement in the trees. Inside their cheeks are flexible pouches where they can temporarily store eucalyptus leaves while feeding.

Their fur isn't just soft—it's a protective coat that helps them survive in changing weather. It keeps them warm during cold nights and sheds water when it rains. Koalas from northern Australia tend to have lighter, thinner fur to stay cool, while southern koalas grow thicker, darker coats for insulation during colder winters.

Where Do Koalas Live?

Koalas live only in the eucalyptus forests of eastern and southeastern Australia. Their range stretches from the tropical woodlands of Queensland to the cooler forests of Victoria and South Australia. These forests give koalas everything they need to survive—food, shelter, and a place to raise their young.

Koalas are arboreal, which means they live in trees. They spend nearly all their time high in the branches, resting, feeding, and sleeping. They prefer forests with tall eucalyptus trees that grow close together, allowing them to move through the canopy without coming down to the ground.

But not all eucalyptus forests are the same. In Queensland, koalas live in warm, humid woodlands with frequent rain and thick tree cover. In southern states like Victoria, the climate is cooler with more open forests and seasonal changes. Koalas in these regions tend to grow larger and have thicker fur to deal with colder winters. The best habitats include a mix of eucalyptus species, healthy soil, and plenty of rainfall—conditions that are becoming harder to find.

The forest floor is also important. It needs to be open enough for young koalas to explore and find new home ranges. But too much clearing—whether from farming, logging, or housing—breaks up the canopy and makes it harder for koalas to move around safely. Roads and fences can trap koalas in small patches of forest, forcing them to cross dangerous ground to find food or mates.

Australia's climate can be harsh, but koalas are built to handle it. On hot summer days, they stretch out in the shade and press their bellies against cool tree trunks to release body heat. During winter, they curl into tight balls in the fork of a tree to stay warm and dry. Their thick fur helps protect them from rain, wind, and extreme temperatures year-round.

Built for Survival – Koala Adaptations

Koalas have some seriously cool body features that make them perfect for life in the eucalyptus forest.

- **Specialized Digestive System:** Koalas can eat eucalyptus leaves that would poison most other animals! They have a special pouch in their intestines filled with bacteria that break down the toxic chemicals in the leaves.

- **Energy-Saving Mode:** Koalas have one of the slowest metabolisms of any mammal. This helps them survive on food that doesn't give much energy.

- **Tree-Climbing Equipment:** Their powerful arms, legs, and sharp claws are perfect for climbing and holding onto trees. Their front paws have two fingers that work like thumbs, giving them an extra-strong grip on branches.

- **Weather-Proof Coat:** A koala's thick, woolly fur keeps it warm in winter, cool in summer, and dry during rainstorms.

- **Tough Bottom:** Koalas have thick cartilage at the end of their spine and special padding on their rear ends. The fur on their rear is also extra thick, which makes it comfortable for them to sit on branches for hours each day.

- **Leaf-Munching:** Koalas have sharp front teeth for cutting leaves and big back teeth for grinding them into pulp. This makes it easier to get nutrients from tough plant material.

- **Water Conservation:** Koalas get almost all their water from eucalyptus leaves. They rarely need to drink from streams or ponds.

- **Compact Brain:** Koalas have relatively small brains that use less energy—another smart adaptation for a low-energy lifestyle.

All these adaptations make koalas perfectly suited to their unique lifestyle in the eucalyptus forests of Australia.

---

adaptations – special body parts or behaviors that help animals survive in their environment

What Do Koalas Eat?

Koalas are incredibly picky eaters with one of the most specialized diets of any mammal on Earth: they eat almost nothing but eucalyptus leaves! Out of more than 800 types of eucalyptus trees in Australia, koalas only eat about 30 to 50 kinds, and they usually have just a few favorite types.

Eucalyptus leaves are tough, fibrous, and don't have many nutrients. They also contain chemicals that would poison most other animals. But koalas have evolved special body features to handle this tricky diet. Their digestive system includes a long pouch called a cecum connected to their intestine. This pouch is filled with helpful bacteria that break down the toxic compounds in eucalyptus leaves.

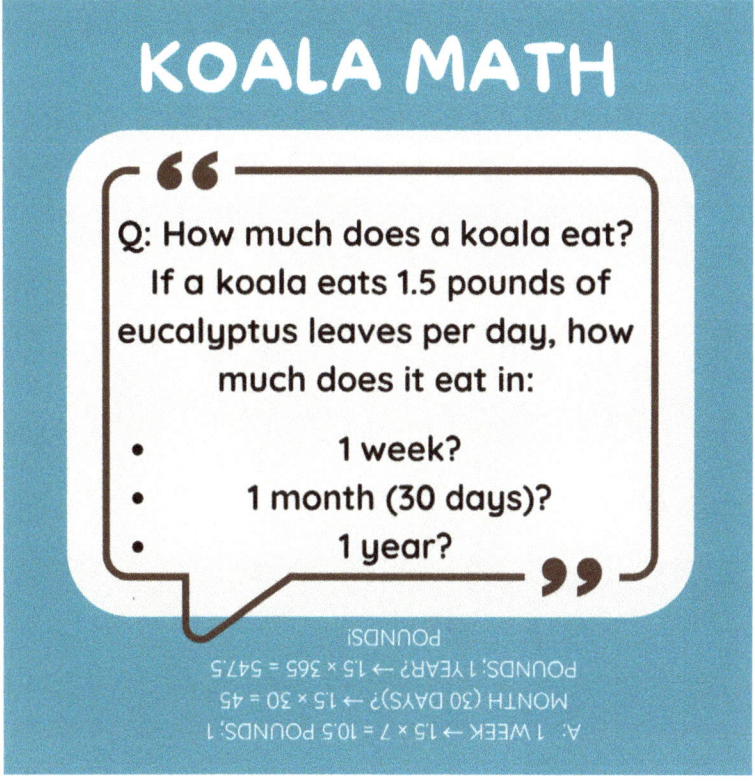

KOALA MATH

Q: How much does a koala eat? If a koala eats 1.5 pounds of eucalyptus leaves per day, how much does it eat in:

- 1 week?
- 1 month (30 days)?
- 1 year?

A: 1 WEEK → 1.5 × 7 = 10.5 POUNDS; 1 MONTH (30 DAYS)? → 1.5 × 30 = 45 POUNDS; 1 YEAR? → 1.5 × 365 = 547.5 POUNDS!

A full-grown koala eats about 1 to 1.5 pounds (0.5 to 0.7 kg) of leaves each day. That's a lot of leaves! They're really choosy about which leaves they munch on, preferring young, tender leaves that have more protein and less fiber. Koalas can tell the difference between leaves from different eucalyptus species just by sniffing them!

Koalas get almost all their water from the eucalyptus leaves they eat. In fact, the name "koala" comes from an Aboriginal word meaning "no drink," because they hardly ever need to drink water. But during droughts or very hot days, koalas will sometimes climb down from trees to drink from streams or water holes.

The low nutritional value of their diet explains their famously relaxed lifestyle—they need to conserve energy!

Life in the Trees

Koalas are solitary animals that generally live alone in their own tree territories. Unlike animals that live in groups, adult koalas prefer their own space most of the time. Each koala claims several eucalyptus trees as their personal territory, marking them with scent to signal to other koalas that the area is occupied.

Though they don't form social groups, koalas do have a social structure. Male koalas have larger territories that often include the smaller territories of several females. During breeding season, males actively seek out females within their range.

QUESTION
What happens to koalas during bushfires?

ANSWER
Bushfires are very dangerous for koalas because they move slowly on the ground. Even when they climb to treetops for safety, intense fires can still reach them. Survivors often need human help until their habitat grows back.

Communication between koalas involves various sounds. Males make loud bellowing calls during mating season that sound like a mix between a snore and a deep growl. This distinctive call can be heard almost a kilometer away and serves to advertise their presence to females and warn competing males. Females also vocalize, especially when they have joeys, making soft clicking, squeaking, and murmuring sounds.

Koalas develop special relationships with their home trees. They recognize which trees offer the best food, shade, and safety. They'll often return to favorite trees repeatedly, and may even have preferred branches for resting.

Young koalas learn essential survival skills from their mothers before becoming independent. This includes learning which eucalyptus species are safe to eat, how to select nutritious leaves, and how to establish territory once they leave their mother's home range.

Despite their solitary nature, koalas in healthy habitats often live in proximity to one another, creating a "neighborhood" of koalas that are aware of each other's presence even without direct social interaction.

Territory and Travel

Koalas don't migrate or travel long distances, but they do have individual home ranges—areas of forest where they live, feed, and sleep. These ranges often overlap, especially in good habitats with lots of eucalyptus trees.

The size of a koala's territory depends on how much food is available. In forests filled with high-quality eucalyptus trees, a koala might only need 2.5 acres (1 hectare)—about the size of a school playground. But in drier or degraded habitats, one koala may need up to 100 acres (40 hectares) to survive. Male koalas usually have larger home ranges than females and may travel longer distances to find mates.

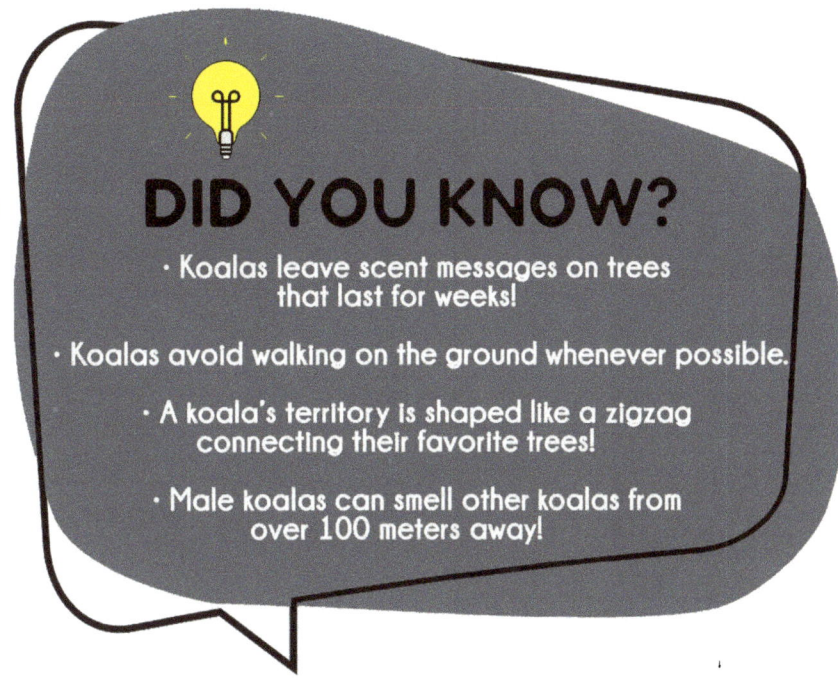

DID YOU KNOW?
- Koalas leave scent messages on trees that last for weeks!
- Koalas avoid walking on the ground whenever possible.
- A koala's territory is shaped like a zigzag connecting their favorite trees!
- Male koalas can smell other koalas from over 100 meters away!

Koalas mark their territory using scent. Males have a gland on their chest that produces a sticky, strong-smelling substance. They rub this scent onto trees to signal that the area is taken. Both males and females also leave scent trails by urinating on tree trunks. These markers help koalas avoid conflict by letting others know who's nearby.

Koalas mostly move between trees in their home range to find better leaves or a more comfortable resting spot. They prefer to travel through the canopy when trees are close together, but when trees are far apart, they're forced to come down and walk across the ground. This is when they're most vulnerable to predators, cars, and dogs.

Sometimes, koalas meet face to face—especially when home ranges overlap or food is scarce. These meetings usually involve grunting, bellowing, or climbing away. Physical fights are rare, but they can happen between males during the breeding season.

A Day in the Life

Koalas are mostly nocturnal, meaning they're active at night. They're also crepuscular, which means they tend to move around during the early morning and late evening hours. During the daytime, koalas rest quietly in the treetops—sometimes sleeping up to 20 hours a day! All that rest helps them conserve energy, since their diet of eucalyptus leaves doesn't provide much fuel.

As the sun goes down, a koala's day begins. They wake up slowly, stretch their limbs, and begin their first meal of the night. Koalas are extremely picky eaters. They carefully sniff and select leaves, choosing younger, softer ones with fewer toxins and more nutrients. It's not a fast meal—koalas chew slowly and thoroughly to get every bit of energy from each bite.

A KOALA'S DAY

- **Evening (5–8 PM)**: Wakes up and starts feeding
- **Night (8 PM–2 AM)**: Climbs trees, eats, and rests
- **Early morning (2–6 AM)**: Final meal and grooming
- **Daytime (6 AM–5 PM)**: Sleeps curled in a tree fork

During the night, koalas might change trees to find better food. They move carefully but confidently through the tree branches, using their strong limbs and sharp claws to keep a solid grip. When necessary, they'll climb down to the ground to walk between trees that aren't connected by branches.

Koalas often take long breaks between feeding sessions, resting in the fork of a tree where they feel safe. They don't need to be constantly alert—koalas have few natural predators and can afford to relax during their active hours.

Before sunrise, most koalas enjoy one last feeding session, then settle into their sleeping spot for the day. They curl up in a sturdy tree fork, tucking their head and limbs in to conserve body heat and stay hidden from danger. It's a quiet, still part of the forest day—koalas blending into the leaves and branches until night returns.

During especially hot weather, koalas may shift their schedule slightly. They might become more active during the cooler hours of early morning or late evening, and they often move to shadier parts of the tree. On very hot days, they may even come down to the ground to rest against the cooler base of a tree trunk.

Mating and Birth

Koalas breed once a year, usually during the Australian summer, from December to March. During this time, the forest becomes much noisier, especially because of the males. Male koalas produce deep, rumbling calls that sound like a mix between a growl and a snore. These bellows can travel more than a kilometer through the forest. They help attract females and warn other males to stay away.

Males often compete for the chance to mate. These encounters may involve chasing, scratching, or pushing, but serious fights are uncommon. Most of the time, the largest or strongest male in the area gets the opportunity to mate.

Female koalas can start having young at about two years old and usually have one baby per year. Twin births almost never happen in koalas. Sometimes they may skip a year if conditions are tough, such as during drought or after raising a joey that needed extra care. Males typically mature later, becoming ready to breed at three to four years old.

A koala's pregnancy lasts only about 35 days—very short compared to most mammals. The baby, called a joey, is born hairless, blind, and extremely small—about the size of a jelly bean. Although tiny and underdeveloped, the joey is strong enough to crawl from the birth canal, through its mother's fur, and into her pouch. Once safety inside, it attaches to one of two teats and stays securely inside while it continues to grow.

> **DID YOU KNOW?**
> - A newborn koala joey is smaller than a jelly bean
> - Baby koalas crawl into their mother's pouch while still blind and hairless
> - Male koalas sometimes fight by pushing and scratching during mating season
> - Twin koala joeys are extremely rare - it almost never happens

Growing Up Koala

A koala joey spends the first 6 to 7 months of life inside its mother's pouch, continuing to grow from a tiny, undeveloped newborn into a fully formed young koala. Around 6 months old, the joey begins peeking out of the pouch, getting its first look at the outside world.

By 7 to 8 months, it has opened its eyes, grown a soft coat of fur, and begins venturing out of the pouch for short periods. If startled, the joey quickly retreats to the safety of the pouch. During this stage, it also begins eating pap, a soft, nutrient-rich form of the mother's droppings. Pap contains the special bacteria needed to help the joey digest eucalyptus leaves, which would otherwise be toxic.

Between 8 and 12 months, the joey becomes too large for the pouch and starts riding on its mother's back or clinging to her belly. It still nurses, but also begins to eat eucalyptus leaves more regularly, learning which trees and leaves to choose by watching its mother.

Growth of a Koala

Newborn   2 months   6 months   12 months

The mother plays an important role as teacher. She shows her joey how to climb safely, find good food, and choose safe places to rest. Young koalas learn by observing and imitating her behavior, gradually gaining confidence and independence.

By about 12 months old, the joey is fully weaned and eating only eucalyptus leaves. It continues to live within its mother's territory for a few more months, practicing the skills it will need to survive on its own.

Between 18 and 36 months of age, most young koalas leave their mothers for good and begin searching for a place to call their own. Female koalas often stay closer to their birthplace, sometimes establishing territories near their mothers. Male koalas usually travel farther, looking for unoccupied forest and avoiding conflicts with older males.

Koalas and Their Ecosystem

Koalas play several important roles in keeping their eucalyptus forest homes healthy and balanced.

- **Forest Health Indicators:** Because koalas depend entirely on eucalyptus forests, changes in their population can signal larger problems in the environment. When koala numbers drop, it may point to issues like habitat loss, pollution, or climate stress. Scientists study koalas as indicator species to better understand the overall health of the forest.

- **Natural Tree Trimmers:** Koalas are selective feeders. By eating specific leaves from eucalyptus trees, they help shape forest growth. Their picky diet encourages new leaf growth and helps keep certain tree species from dominating the ecosystem.

- **Nutrient Recyclers:** Koalas return nutrients to the forest through their droppings. As their waste breaks down, it adds important minerals to the soil—especially valuable in Australia, where soils are often low in nutrients.

- **Support for Other Species:** Many other animals—including gliders, cockatoos, owls, frogs, and insects—rely on the same eucalyptus forests that koalas call home. Efforts to protect koalas and their habitat also help these species survive.

- **Cultural and Economic Importance:** Koalas are one of Australia's most famous animals. Their popularity draws tourists and raises awareness, which can help generate funding for conservation. Protecting koalas often leads to protection of entire ecosystems.

- **Flagship Species for Conservation:** Because koalas are so well-known and widely loved, they serve as a flagship species. This means they represent broader conservation efforts. Saving koalas also brings attention to the many other species and systems that share their habitat.

- **Research Opportunities:** Koalas help scientists learn more about forest ecosystems. Studying their diet, reproduction, and adaptation to toxic plants helps researchers understand how animals interact with the environment—and how to better protect it.

By focusing on protecting koalas and the eucalyptus forests they need to survive, conservationists also protect the biodiversity and long-term health of eastern Australia's ecosystems.

Natural Predators

Adult koalas have few natural enemies, thanks to their tree-dwelling lifestyle and ability to stay still and hidden in the forest canopy. But that doesn't mean they're completely safe in the wild—especially when they come down to the ground or when young koalas are on their own for the first time.

Large birds of prey, like powerful owls and wedge-tailed eagles, may occasionally hunt young koalas. These birds usually target smaller animals, but juvenile koalas—especially those that have just left their mothers—can be vulnerable if they're not yet skilled at spotting or avoiding danger.

Dingoes and wild dogs are more serious threats, particularly when koalas are forced to travel on the ground between trees. In areas where forests have been cleared or broken up, this kind of ground travel becomes more common. Carpet pythons, large snakes found in parts of Australia, may also prey on young koalas or small adults.

Koalas are at their most vulnerable when walking. On the ground, they move with a slow, waddling gait and can't escape quickly if threatened. This is why they prefer to stay in the trees and only come down when absolutely necessary.

Despite these risks, adult koalas living in healthy, connected forests are usually able to avoid predators. Their excellent sense of hearing, wide field of vision, and strong climbing abilities help them detect danger and quickly return to the safety of the treetops.

For young koalas, especially those just beginning life on their own, the risks are higher. Without the protection of their mother, they must learn to avoid predators while searching for food, shelter, and a home of their own.

Threats and Challenges

In addition to natural predators, koalas face many serious dangers—most of them caused by humans.

Habitat Loss: The greatest threat to koalas is the destruction of their eucalyptus forest homes. Land is often cleared for cities, roads, farming, or logging. As forests are cut down or divided by buildings and highways, koalas lose their food trees and shelter. In fragmented habitats, they are forced to travel on the ground more often, which puts them at greater risk from cars, dogs, and heat.

Disease: A bacterial infection called chlamydia affects many wild koalas. It can cause blindness, infertility, and even death. Koalas under stress, like those that have lost their habitat, are more likely to get sick because their immune systems are weakened. Scientists are working on treatments and vaccines, but it remains a major threat.

Car Accidents: As human development expands, roads often cut through koala territory. Koalas moving between forest patches may be hit by cars, especially at night. Thousands of koalas are injured or killed in vehicle collisions each year.

Dog Attacks: Pet dogs and wild dogs pose a serious danger to koalas, especially in areas where neighborhoods and koala habitat overlap. Koalas are most at risk when they are on the ground moving between trees.

Climate Change: Rising temperatures and changing rainfall patterns affect the quality of eucalyptus leaves, sometimes making them less nutritious. More frequent and severe droughts can also reduce the water content in leaves, forcing koalas to look for water elsewhere. Intense heatwaves can be deadly, especially for koalas that can't find shade or moisture.

Bushfires: Wildfires have always been part of Australia's natural environment, but climate change is making them more frequent and more severe. Fires can move quickly through eucalyptus forests, leaving koalas with no way to escape.

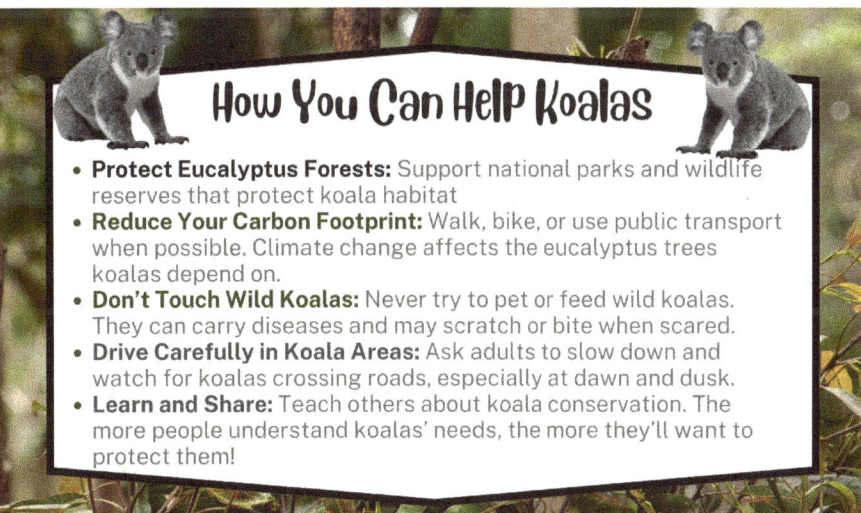

How You Can Help Koalas

- **Protect Eucalyptus Forests:** Support national parks and wildlife reserves that protect koala habitat
- **Reduce Your Carbon Footprint:** Walk, bike, or use public transport when possible. Climate change affects the eucalyptus trees koalas depend on.
- **Don't Touch Wild Koalas:** Never try to pet or feed wild koalas. They can carry diseases and may scratch or bite when scared.
- **Drive Carefully in Koala Areas:** Ask adults to slow down and watch for koalas crossing roads, especially at dawn and dusk.
- **Learn and Share:** Teach others about koala conservation. The more people understand koalas' needs, the more they'll want to protect them!

Koalas are resilient animals, but they face more challenges now than ever before. Conservation efforts—like protecting forests, building wildlife corridors, supporting rescue and research programs, and educating communities—are key to helping koalas survive and recover.

Lifespan and Population

In the wild, koalas usually live about 10 to 12 years. In wildlife parks or zoos, where they receive veterinary care and are protected from predators and disease, they may live up to 15 years or more. Female koalas tend to live longer than males, partly because males often travel more and compete during breeding season.

Koala populations have dropped sharply over the past hundred years. Before European settlement, there were likely millions of koalas across eastern Australia. But between 1890 and 1927, millions were killed for their fur, and by the early 1900s, the species was nearly wiped out in some areas. Although hunting koalas is now banned, they still face major threats—including habitat loss, car accidents, disease, and the growing impacts of climate change.

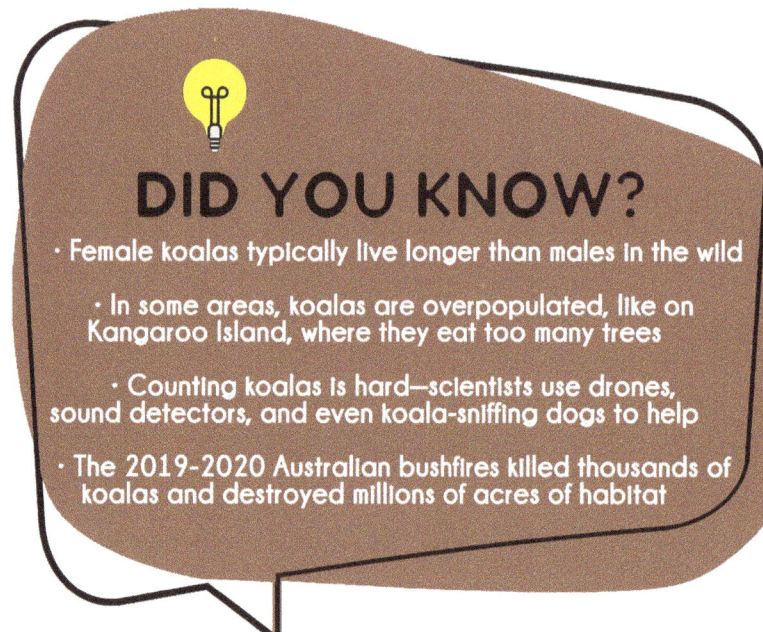

DID YOU KNOW?
- Female koalas typically live longer than males in the wild
- In some areas, koalas are overpopulated, like on Kangaroo Island, where they eat too many trees
- Counting koalas is hard—scientists use drones, sound detectors, and even koala-sniffing dogs to help
- The 2019-2020 Australian bushfires killed thousands of koalas and destroyed millions of acres of habitat

Today, scientists estimate that between 40,000 and 100,000 koalas remain in the wild. Getting an exact count is difficult because koalas are solitary animals that live spread out across large areas. Researchers use tracking devices, drones, and habitat surveys to monitor their numbers.

In 2022, the Australian government listed koalas as endangered in Queensland, New South Wales, and the Australian Capital Territory. This was a major change from their earlier status of "vulnerable," which they had held since 2012. In contrast, koala populations in Victoria and South Australia are more stable, and in some small, isolated areas, even overabundant. However, even these populations face risks from habitat changes and disease.

Koalas are now distributed in scattered patches across their historic range. In some areas, numbers have dropped quickly due to deforestation and development. In others, careful habitat management has helped populations hold steady. The biggest factors affecting koala numbers today are habitat quality, disease, road networks, and how much land remains connected and protected.

Conservation efforts are critical to keeping koala populations healthy. These efforts include protecting eucalyptus forests, building wildlife corridors to reconnect habitats, researching disease, improving road safety, and educating the public. Without continued action, experts warn that koalas could disappear from large parts of their range within the next few decades.

The Future of Koalas

Throughout this book, we've explored what makes koalas such extraordinary and unique animals. From their treetop lifestyle to their ability to survive on a diet of eucalyptus leaves, koalas show us how wildlife can adapt in remarkable ways to their environment.

Koalas are full of surprises. Although they spend most of the day sleeping, they are perfectly suited for life in the forest canopy. Their strong limbs, sharp claws, and two opposable digits on each front paw allow them to grip branches and climb with ease. Their thick, weather-resistant fur protects them from cold and rain, while their strong sense of smell helps them find just the right leaves to eat. Koalas even have fingerprints so similar to humans that they can be difficult to tell apart.

These quiet marsupials also play an important role in the health of eucalyptus forests. By feeding on select leaves and returning nutrients to the soil, koalas help shape the forest around them. Because they rely so heavily on specific trees and habitat conditions, changes in koala populations can signal trouble in the broader ecosystem.

While koalas face many challenges today, including habitat loss, disease, and extreme weather, there is still reason for hope. Across Australia, conservation groups, scientists, and communities are working to protect forest habitats, care for injured koalas, and create safer spaces where wild populations can recover and grow.

Koalas remind us that the choices people make—about land, wildlife, and climate—have a lasting impact. Protecting koalas also means protecting the many other animals and plants that share their forests.

Through their resilience, gentle presence, and deep connection to the Australian landscape, koalas inspire us to care for the natural world. They are a symbol of what is at stake—and what can still be saved.

Word Search

```
L A N R U T C O N S N Y S P E
A A I L A R T S U A O B S D L
R V P U D Q A T K T I E M P P
B X A O Y P P Q B D T F E H R
O G E W P Y T K F Q A I T T E
R T X H L U C G L Y V L S S D
E J E A G K L N J P R D Y E A
A C C R V C I A E T E L S R T
L U W B R Y M Y T D S I O O O
E M H N D I A T H I N W C F R
A D A P T A T I O N O B E A S
L F V G N S E O G L C N M V H
Z E W U A J C N R P H H V F Z
J P A L D E H W S Y C A O N A
O A A V K M A R S U P I A L S
J O U M E D N J O E Y S W O B
K E S F F S G P T A T I B A H
Y G R E N E E S P E C I E S J
```

Adaptation   Eucalyptus   Nocturnal
Arboreal   Forest   Population
Australia   Habitat   Pouch
Climate Change   Joeys   Predators
Conservation   Koalas   Species
Ecosystem   Leaves   Territory
Energy   Marsupials   Wildlife

34

Resources and References

- Australian Koala Foundation. Koala Conservation. 2023, www.savethekoala.com. Accessed 16 May 2025.

- Bass, Cathie. Koalas: The Ultimate Koala Book for Kids. Blue Creek Books, 2020.

- Department of Agriculture, Water and the Environment. National Recovery Plan for the Koala (Phascolarctos cinereus). Australian Government, Mar. 2022, www.dcceew.gov.au/sites/default/files/documents/recovery-plan-koala-2022.pdf. Accessed 16 May 2025.

- Ferguson, Nicola. Koalas. Heinemann Library, 2013.

- Ganeri, Anita. Koala. QEB Publishing, 2021.

- Koala Conservation Australia. About Koalas. 2023, koalaconservationaustralia.org.au/pages/about-koalas. Accessed 16 May 2025.

- National Geographic Kids. "Koalas." National Geographic Kids, 2023, kids.nationalgeographic.com/animals/mammals/facts/koala. Accessed 16 May 2025.

- Paterson, Allison. I Wonder Why Koalas Have Fingerprints and Other Questions About Australia. Kingfisher, 2022.

- Rogers, Kara. Koala: Phascolarctos Cinereus. Britannica Educational Publishing, 2011.

- World Wildlife Fund Australia. Koala Recovery. 2023, www.wwf.org.au/what-we-do/species/koala. Accessed 16 May 2025.

Published by Dylanna Press an imprint of Dylanna Publishing, Inc.
Copyright © 2025 by Dylanna Press
Author: Tyler Grady
All rights reserved. No part of this publication may be reproduced, stored in a retrieval system, or transmitted by any means, including electronic, mechanical, photocopying, or otherwise, without prior written permission of the publisher.

Although the publisher has taken all reasonable care in the preparation of this book, we make no warranty about the accuracy or completeness of its content and, to the maximum extent permitted, disclaim all liability arising from its use.

www.ingramcontent.com/pod-product-compliance
Lightning Source LLC
Chambersburg PA
CBHW040224040426
42333CB00051B/3447